A Practical Approach to Rudimental Drumming

LOW DOWN PUBLISHING

Carmen Intorre Jr.

©2023

ISBN-13: 978-1-7353277-4-7

Editing: John Mills
Cover Design: Alison Coté
Interior Layout: Kelly DiBernardo Rupert
Notation Engraving: Marc Schwartz

Foreword by
Lewis Nash

For more about the author, visit
www.carmenintorrejr.com

Acknowledgements

I want to acknowledge my parents, Carmen Intorre Sr. for his support, encouragement and for being my number one fan and Joan Intorre for her unwavering love that shines down on me from above; Danny Ziemann, John Mills and everyone from Low Down Publishing that helped make this book a reality; Lewis Nash, Mike Clark, Billy Drummond, Adam Nussbaum, Justin DiCioccio, Jason Brown, Steve Fidyk, Matt Wilson, Tom Cohen, Ulysses Owens Jr. and all of my friends and students that have read through the drafts; Steve Maxwell; everyone at Craviotto, DW, Sabian, Promark, Evans, and Lp; all of my teachers throughout my career, and the players that inspire us all.

I'd like to dedicate this book to my wife Gina and my son Jake. Thank you for your constant support, encouragement, and love.

Contents

Foreword

CONGRATULATIONS! With the acquisition of this book, you have taken an important step toward increased facility, independence, confidence and clarity of expression.

In the fall of 2001, I'd just started teaching at Juilliard during the inception of the jazz studies program and in the aftermath of the September 11th tragedy. Carmen Intorre Jr. was one of two drummers in the very first class of the Juilliard jazz program (the other was Ulysses Owens Jr. ... two "Jr.s")!

Besides the fact that he was already very talented, Carmen committed himself to putting in the time and work required to facilitate growth. Since that time, I've been able to observe his application of so many of the concepts and techniques we discussed and worked on back then. His consistent presence on the scene and stellar drumming on the many tours and recordings he's done are a testament to his understanding of the history, role and importance of the drums in various musical situations.

With this book, Carmen puts the emphasis on "practical". As he explains in the introduction, he selected rudiments he found himself playing most often in professional settings. This highlights the fact that we can view rudiments similarly to the way an artist might view various paint colors or colored pencils. Which rudiments may be applicable in a given situation can vary depending on the groove or feel (swinging, Afro 6/8, samba, calypso, R&B/funk, triplet subdivision vs. duple, etc), meter or tempo. Years of touring and playing a variety of music with high level bands has given Carmen first hand insight into applying the rudiments in a practical yet creative way.

I'm particularly fond of his section called "Travel Exercises". These are designed to help develop facility in executing the rudiments ('traveling") around the drum set. Please remember however, that expanded rudimental facility is not the end goal! The increased facility makes possible the clear and precise execution of improvised rhythmic ideas (from simple to complex) in each musical moment (comping, timekeeping, reacting and responding). This facility is important in playing a more "melodic" or "linear" style of drum solo as well.

Once again, congratulations and prepare to enjoy your journey with Carmen Intorre Jr. to a more creative and practical use of rudiments!

— Lewis Nash

Introduction

So, you want to play drums? Maybe you'd like to enhance your skills or even start to study this instrument? Well, I think that you have come to the right place to learn. I believe that in order to really learn the drums we must have a strong foundation. Having a solid foundation will enable you to grow and achieve your goals on the drums. In order to have a strong foundation you must learn the rudiments. Think of learning rudiments in the same way pianists and other instrumentalists learn scales.

All of the greats such as Buddy Rich, Max Roach, Roy Haynes, Philly Joe Jones, Elvin Jones, Art Blakey, Jimmy Cobb, Tony Williams, Billy Cobham, Steve Gadd, John Bonham, Peter Erskine, Mike Clark, David Garibaldi, Dennis Chambers, Vinnie Colaiuta, Dave Weckl, and many others all have one thing in common: they all have mastered playing rudiments. Now I know that being told to learn your rudiments can be a drag but they are crucial in many ways. I wrote this book in hopes that these exercises will inspire you without the burden of learning.

For this book I choose ten essential rudiments that I find myself playing often in professional settings. Subsequent volumes in this series will address other rudiments and their applications. This book is written to teach you practical ways of learning your rudiments and to give you ideas on how to make music around the drums in any situation.

I hope this book will enhance your skills in a positive and practical way. Be patient with yourself, go step by step, and study hard! You will be amazed with your improvements!

How to Practice

You may have the urge to jump right in and go for it, but I feel it is very important to have a practice routine with goals in mind. When practicing, you should work on the things that you have trouble with. Playing what you already know is ok, but it will not maximize your practice time or help you learn new things. For me, I believe in practicing slowly and gradually working the tempo up. This strategy will not only help you break down the exercises but will often give you clarity. Remember there is nothing difficult; it is either familiar or unfamiliar.

When playing through these exercises, give yourself a chance to really learn them. Pay close attention to the sticking indicated and alternate when possible, practice beat by beat, bar by bar, and start to add the following bars until you feel absolutely comfortable with the exercise. Then move on to the next exercise.

I also highly recommend recording yourself while practicing so that you can hear exactly what you sound like. Remember to take your time and be patient with yourself. You will be amazed with your development if you practice this way.

Have fun!

Carmen Intorre Jr.

Section 1
Warm-Up Exercises

Warming up on the drums is very important. Before each practice session I recommend warming up for 5-10 minutes. These exercises will help you relax and give you a chance to focus on your stick height, sound, sticking, and overall sense of warming up your hands. Practice slow, keep the unaccented notes low to the drum (about an inch off the drum) and exaggerate the accented notes. Pay close attention to the sticking (rights "R" and lefts "L").

(Set your metronome to ♩ = 60 and when you feel very comfortable, move the speed up. Various speeds at slow- medium- fast- are recommended. I also like to keep time with my feet by playing the bass drum on all four beats and the hi-hat on beats two and four. Like this:

1a.

1b.

2a.

2b.

3a.

3b.

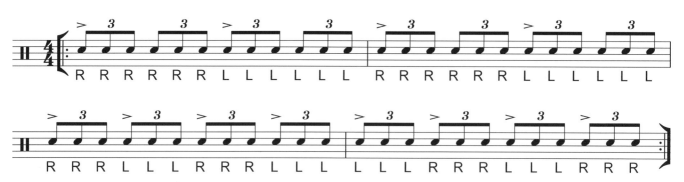

4a.

R R R R R R R R R R R R R R R R   L L L L L L L L L L L L L L L L

R R R R R R R R R R R L L L L   L L L L L L L L R R L L R R L L

4b.

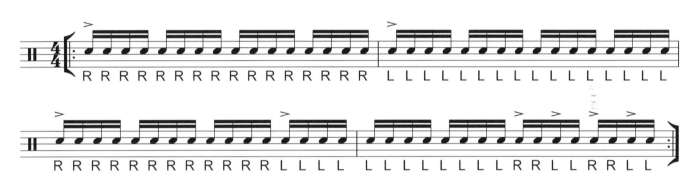

R R R R R R R R R R R R R R R R   L L L L L L L L L L L L L L L L

R R R R R R R R R R R L L L L   L L L L L L L L R R L L R R L L

Section 2
10 Essential Rudiments

I chose these ten rudiments to give you a proper introduction to playing them, and also to challenge you in positive ways. It is important to pay attention to the sticking and close attention to the accented and unaccented notes, because it is these articulations that give these rudiments their identities.

Set your metronome to ♩ = 60 and when you feel very comfortable, increase the speed. Various speeds at slow- medium-, fast- tempos are recommended. I also like to keep time with my feet by playing the bass drum on all four beats, and the hi-hat on beats two and four.

Single Stroke Roll

R L R L R L R L R L R L R L R L R L R L R L R L R L R L R L

Double Stroke Roll

R R L L R R L L R R L L R R L L R R L L R R L L RRLL RRLL

5 Stroke Roll

R R L L R R L L R R L R R L L R L L R R L RRLLR LLRRL RRLLR LLRRL RRLLR LLRRL

7 Stroke Roll

R R L L R R L R R L L R R L R R L L R R L R R L L R R L RRLLRRL RRLLRRL RRLLRRL RRLLRRL
L L R R L L R L L R R L L R L L R R L L R L L R R L L R LLRRLLR LLRRLLR LLRRLLR LLRRLLR

Single Paradiddle

R L R R L R L L R L R R L R L L R L R R L R L L R L R R L R L L

Double Paradiddle

R L R L R R L R L R L L R L R L R R L R L R L L R L R L R R L R L R L L R L R L R R

Flam

LR RL LR RL LR RL LR RL LR RL LR RL LR RL LR RL LR RL LR RL LR RL LR RL

Flam Accent

LR L R RL R L LR L R RL R L LR L R RL R L LR L R RL R L

Drag

LLR RRL LLR RRL LLR RRL LLR RRL LLR RRL LLR RRL LLR RRL LLR RRL

Single Drag Tap

LLR L RRL R LLR L RRL R LLR L RRL R LLR L RRL R

Section 3
Rudimental Exercises

I have written ten different exercises for each of the ten essential rudiments. For each exercise, I have written a two-bar phrase that uses the same sticking as its corresponding rudiment. Pay close attention to the accented and unaccented notes, sticking, and rhythms. I like to practice these by playing each exercise one bar at a time. When you feel comfortable, add the next bar to complete the phrase.

Set your metronome to ♩ = 60 and when you feel very comfortable move the speed up. Various speeds at slow- medium- fast are recommended. I also like to keep time with my feet by playing the bass drum on all four beats and the hi hat on beats two and four. Like this:

Single Stroke Roll Exercises

Double Stroke Roll Exercises

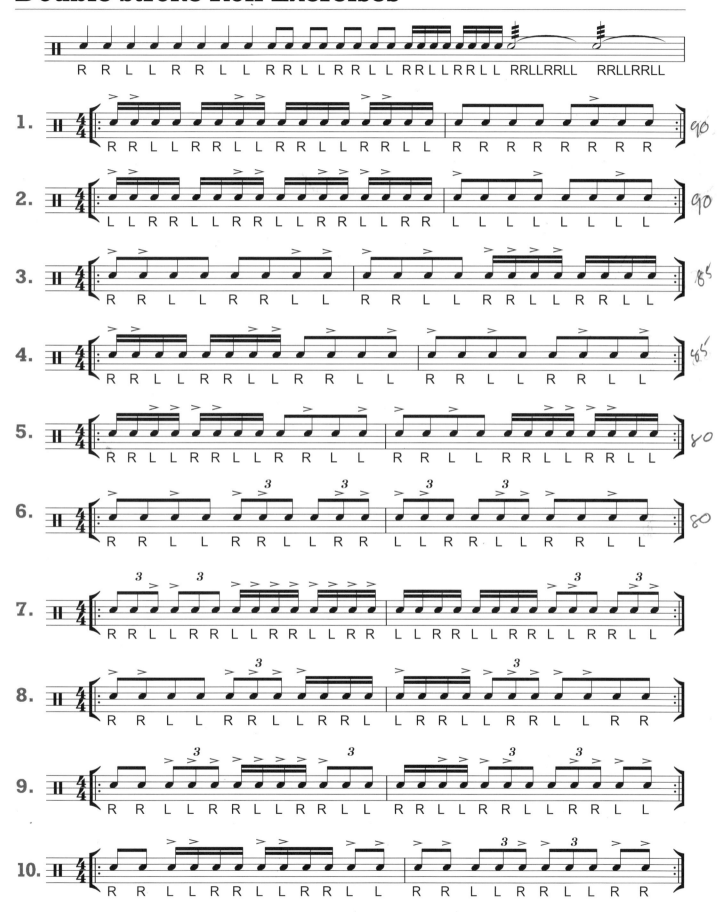

5 Stroke Roll Exercises

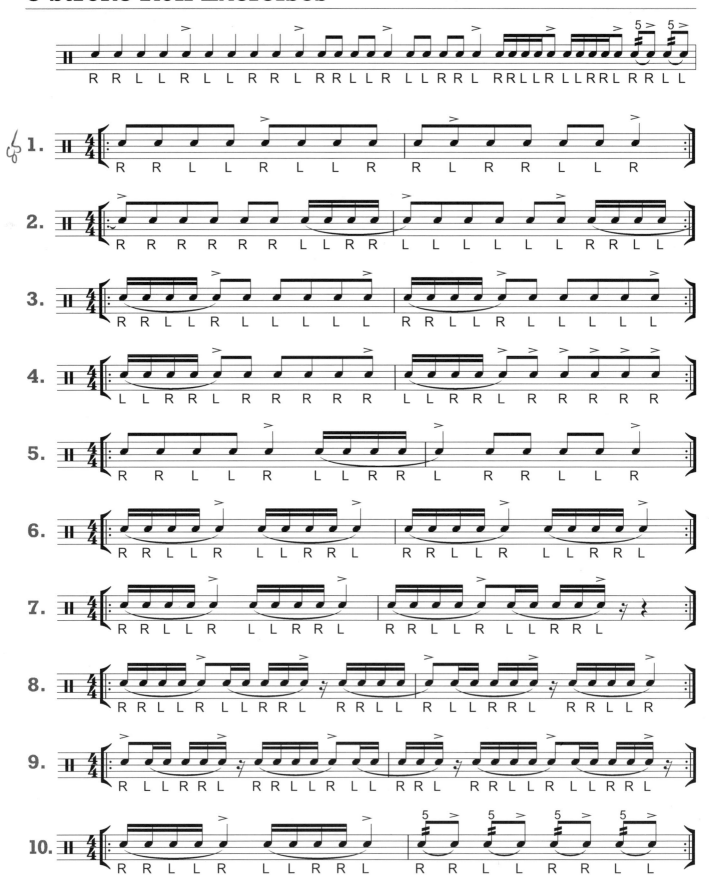

7 Stroke Roll Exercises

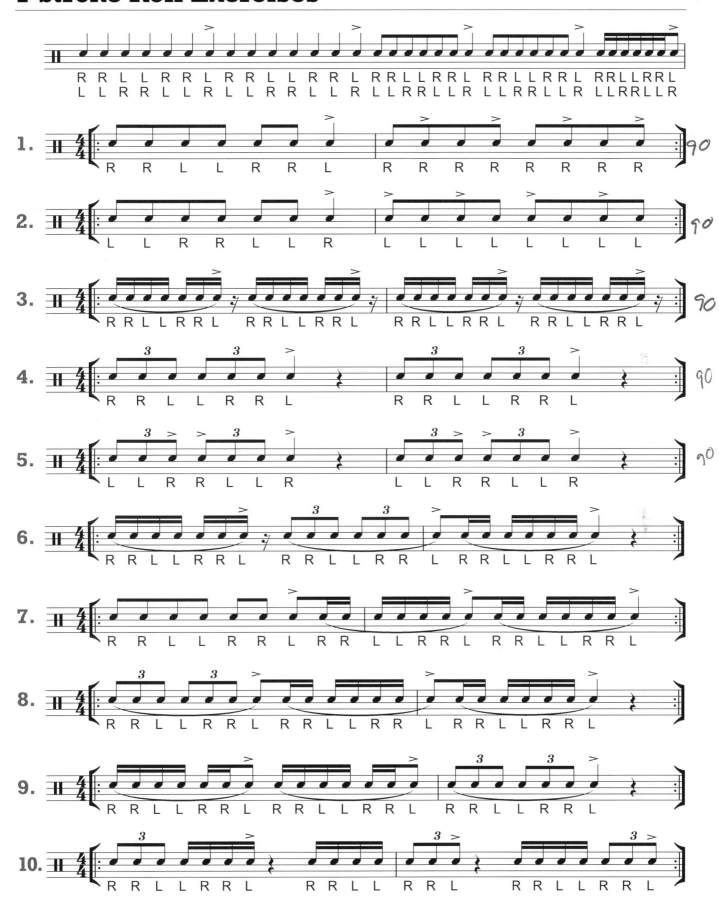

Single Paradiddle Exercises

R L R R L R L L R L R R L R L L R L R R L R L L

1.

2.

3.

4.

5.

6.

7.

8.

9.

10.

Double Paradiddle Exercises

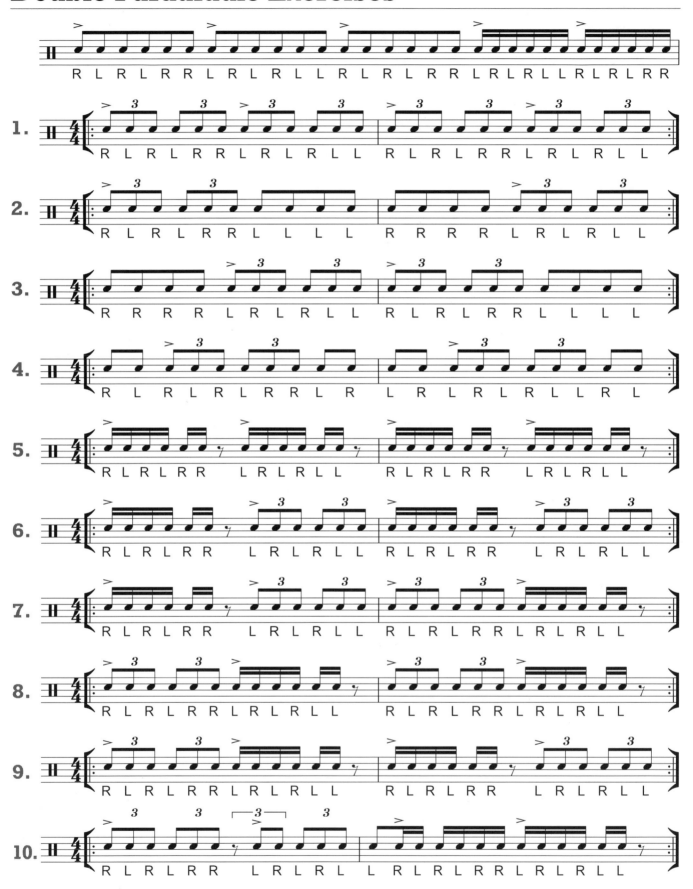

Flam Exercises

Flam Accent Exercises

Drag Exercises

9.

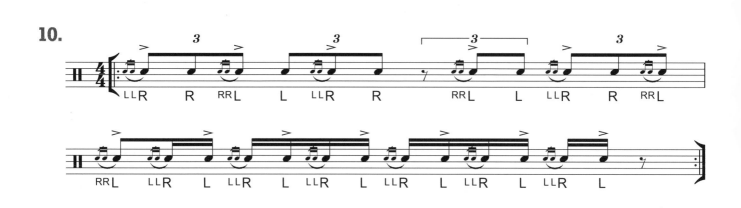

10.

Single Drag Tap Exercises

Section 4
Travel Exercises

In this section, we start to incorporate the previous exercises within the drum set. All right-hand accents are played on the floor tom, and all left-hand accents are played on the tom tom. The unaccented notes are played on the snare drum. It is very important to follow the sticking indicated. I call these exercises "travel exercises" because you will begin to orchestrate rudiments around the drum set and start to play melodic ideas.

Drum Set Key

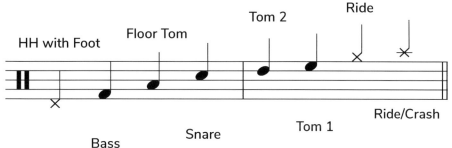

Single Stroke Roll Travel Exercises

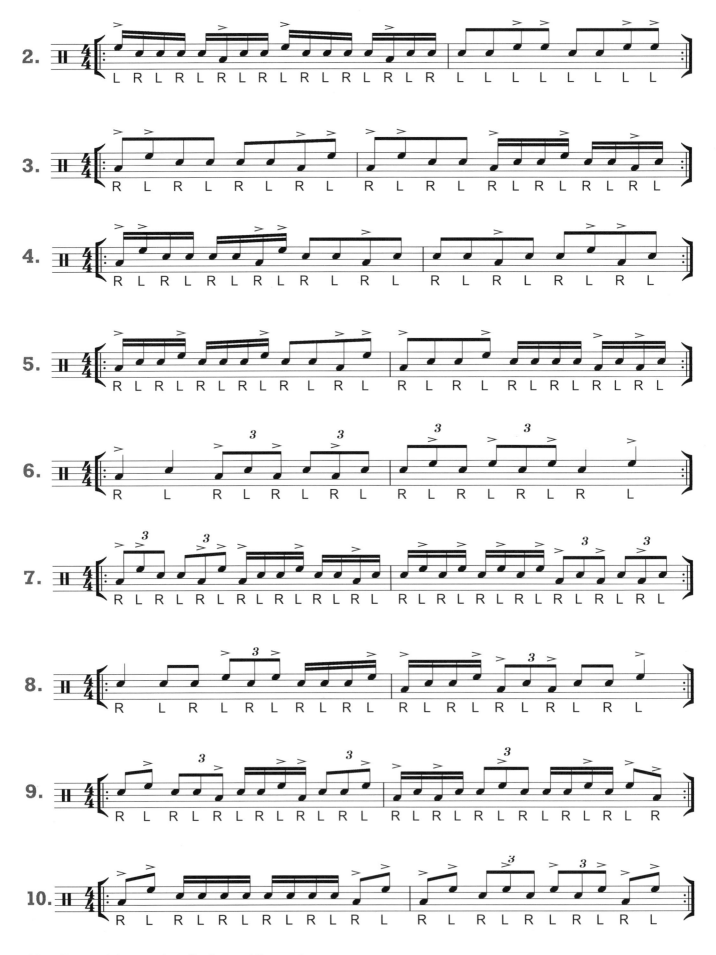

Double Stroke Roll Travel Exercises

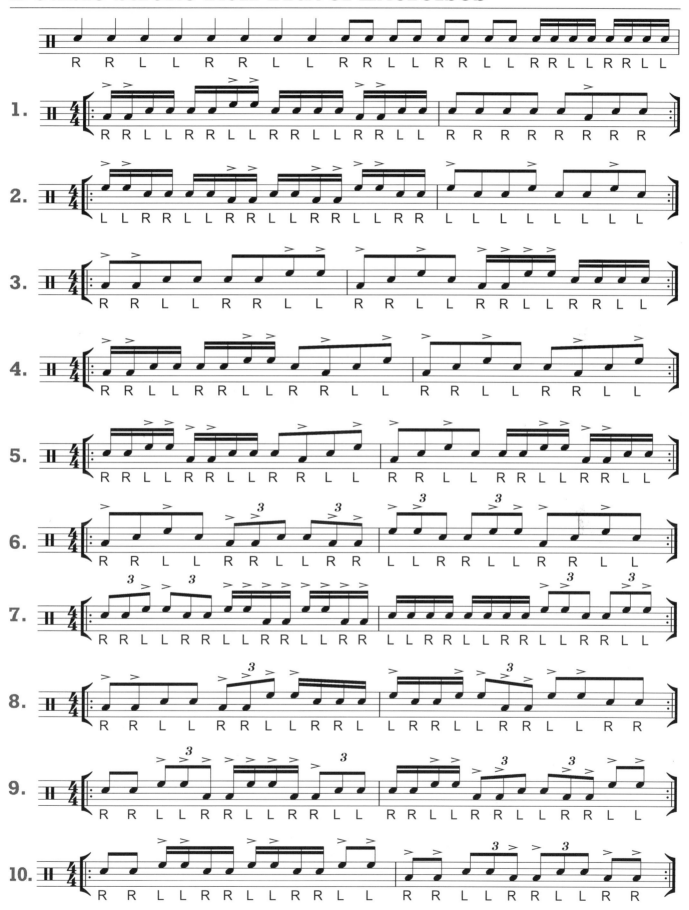

5 Stroke Roll Travel Exercises

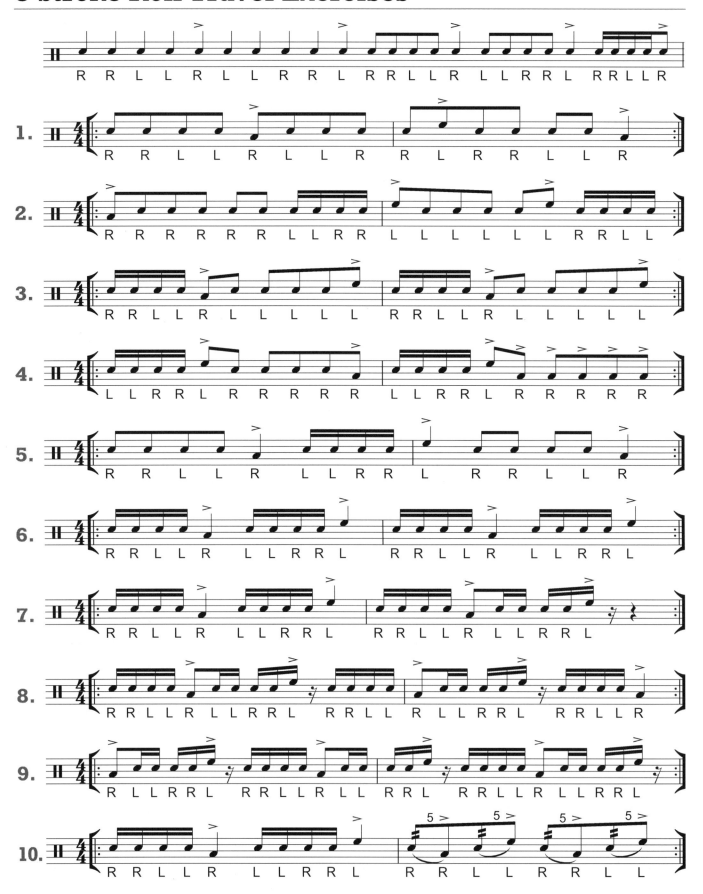

7 Stroke Roll Travel Exercises

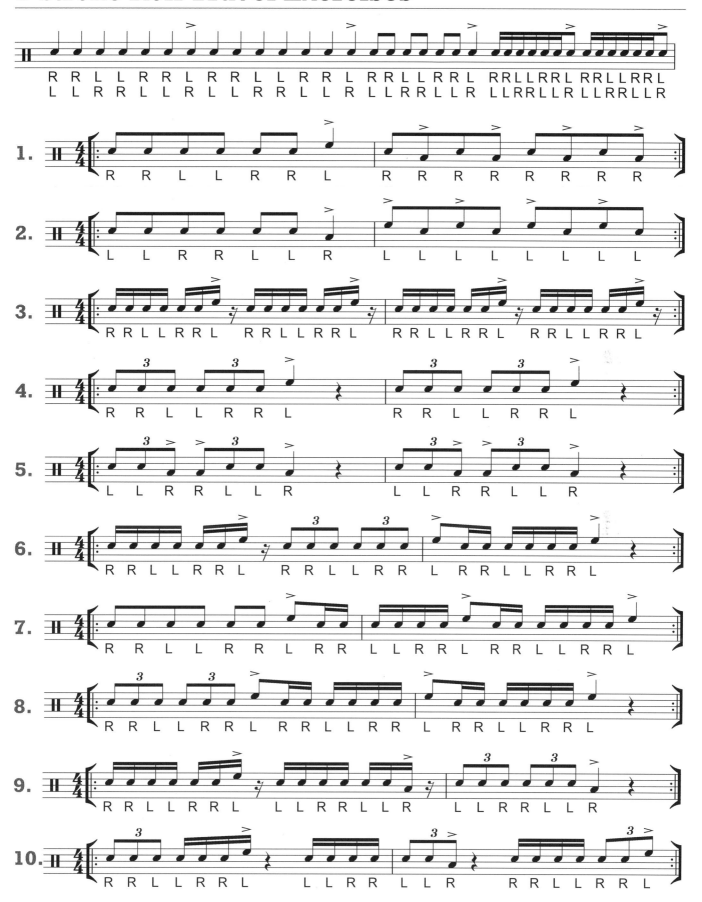

Single Paradiddle Travel Exercises

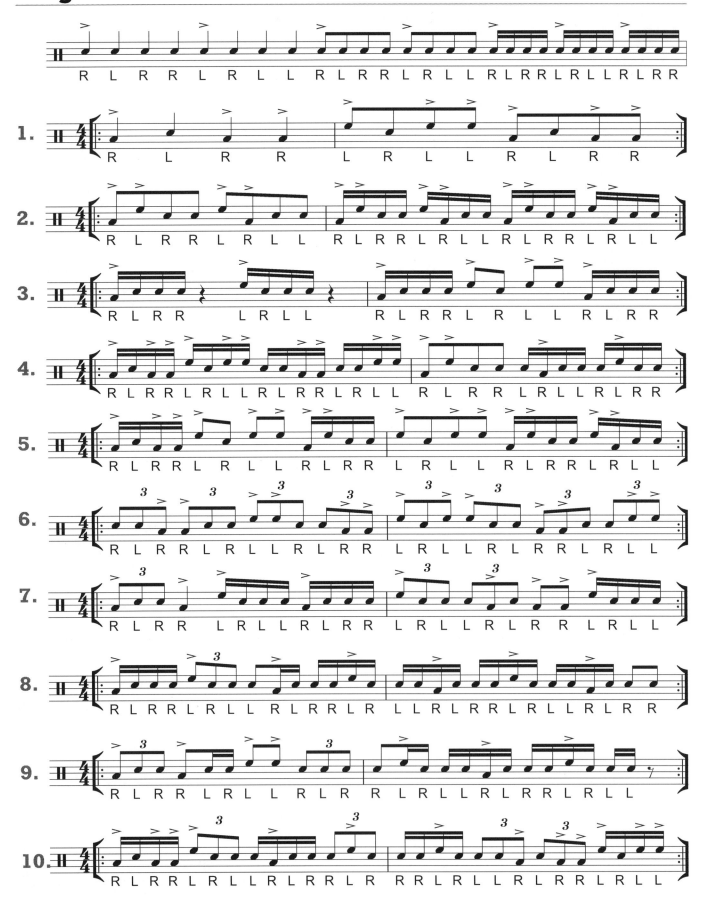

Double Paradiddle Travel Exercises

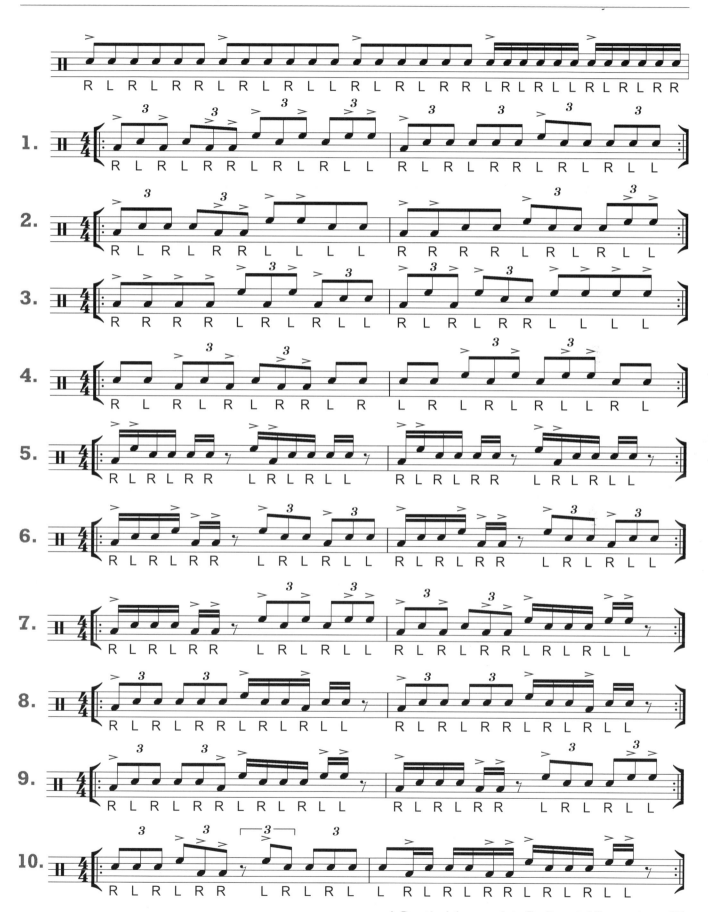

Flam Travel Exercises

Flam Accent Travel Exercises

Drag Travel Exercises

Single Drag Travel Exercises

Section 5
Rudimental Applications for the Drum Set

We will use all of the exercises learned in Sections 3 and 4 and start to incorporate them on the drum set in various ways. Remember to use the correct sticking and to keep time on the bass drum and hi-hat. For me, I like to base my emphasis on the swing (jazz) rhythm but feel free to use any rhythm you would like.

These are some of the ways I like to use in my own playing, and this practice allows me to come up with more ideas and build vocabulary I can use in professional situations. These applications are by no means the end all; the possibilities are endless.

I hope practicing these applications will help you

- play around the kit,
- develop more vocabulary,
- start to hear the drums played more melodically,
- get out of your comfort zone, and
- encourage you to use your imagination to come up with your own ways to play.

Drum Set Key

Basic Rhythms

Swing (Jazz Styles)

Even 8th Note Styles

Latin Styles

Remember to use the correct sticking and to keep time on the bass drum and hi-hat.

1. Play 4 bars of time (rhythm) and 4 bars of the exercise as written.

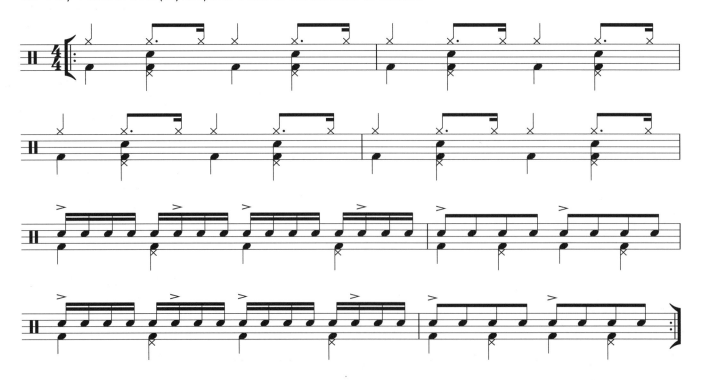

2. Play 4 bars of time, then 4 bars of the exercise while traveling the accents.

3. Play 4 bars of time, then one bar on each drum: first bar on the snare, second bar on tom 1, third bar on tom 2, fourth bar on the floor tom.

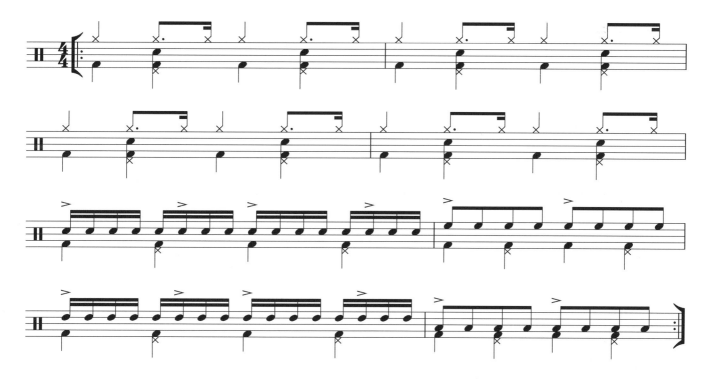

4. Play 4 bars of time, then a different drum on every two beats.

5. Play 4 bars of time, then play the right hand accents on the ride cymbal along with the bass drum.
And play the left-hand accents on the crash/ride cymbal along with the bass drum.

6. Play 4 bars of time, then play the accents only on the snare drum and hand-to-hand on the toms. Remember to always follow the original sticking

7. Bonus: Play 4 bars of time, then play the accented rhythm in your left hand while continuing to play time (swing rhythm in this case). When you look at each exercise, try to isolate only the accented notes which will give you a new rhythm/exercise.

*The new rhythm/exercise will become this:

Section 6
Drum Solos

In this section are five drum solos. There are various ways to practice and explore them, including the ways we have learned throughout this book.

To recap hand-to-hand, travel the accents, accented rhythm in the left hand, and other ways that you have come up with on your own.

Each of these solos are 32 bars. This means you can also approach them within AABA song form

- A section = the melody
- B section = the bridge
- Each section = 8 bars, Adding up to 32 total bars.

Take a block of 4 bars, 8 bars, or sections and trade with yourself by playing time, and playing the block of bars as your solo. Remember to play time for the same number of bars as the solo you choose to block out.

The possibilities are endless!

Solo #1

Combining single stroke roll and double stroke roll

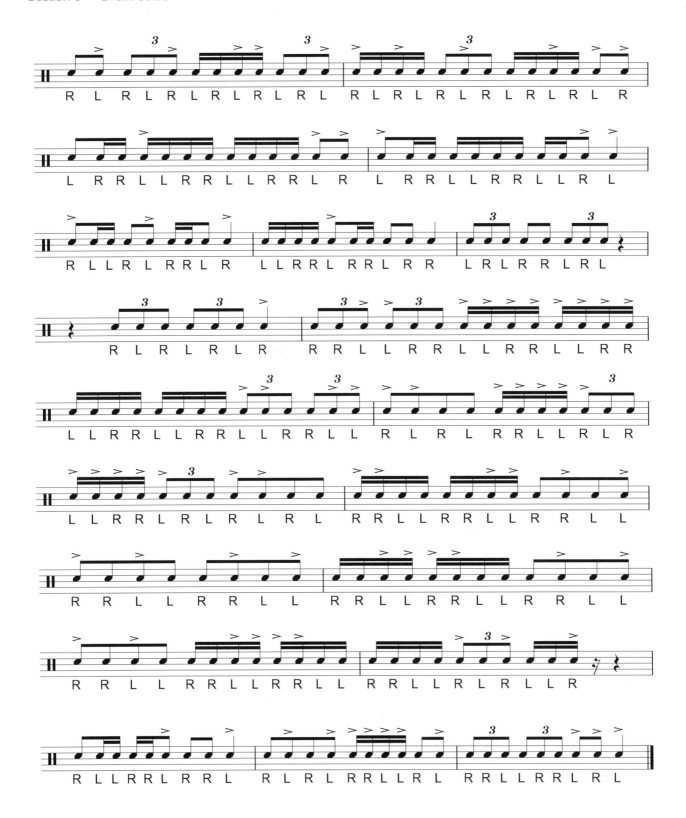

Solo #2

Combining 5 stroke roll and 7 stroke roll

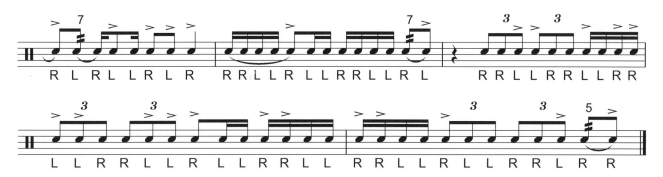

Solo #3

Combining single paradiddle and double paradiddle

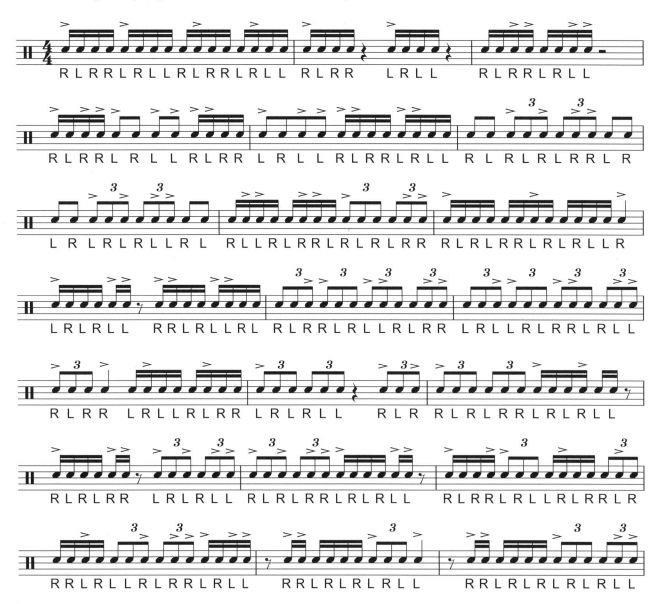

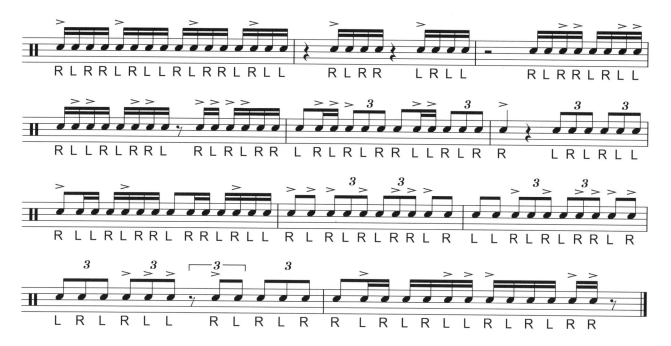

Solo #4

Combining flam and flam accent

Solo #5

Combining drag and single drag tap

About the Author

Carmen Intorre Jr. developed an early interest in music and has been playing and studying the drums for the past 35 years. He has studied with Gary Rutkowski, Louie Marino, Billy Hart, Michael Carvin, Lewis Nash, Carl Allen, Jimmy Cobb, Billy Drummond, and Kenny Washington.

Receiving both his BM and MM degrees from The Juilliard School, Intorre is always eager to uncover the latest information about music and drumming and to share that information with others. For the past 20 years he has given masterclasses and clinics throughout the world including the United States, Canada, Colombia, Costa Rica, Spain, Italy, Germany, Japan, and Thailand. In addition to teaching at colleges, universities, high schools, and music camps, Intorre has also developed a successful private studio where he teaches individual and group lessons for students of all ages and levels in percussion, drum set, and Latin percussion instruments. Intorre states, "This is my job. I have to give back what I was given a chance to do. Music is an opportunity for me to give up my soul, while in the process connecting with the students' souls as well."

Intorre has performed and recorded with musicians such as George Benson, Larry Coryell, Joey DeFrancesco, Wynton Marsalis, Monty Alexander, George Coleman, Dr. Lonnie Smith, Eric Alexander, George Cables, Benny Golson, Richie Cole, Joe Locke, Lew Tabackin, Bobby Watson, Ira Sullivan, Bucky Pizzarelli, Pee Wee Ellis, Bennie Wallace, Mike LeDonne, Reuben Wilson, and many others. For eight years, Intorre toured the world as part of legendary jazz guitarist Pat Martino's Trio and Quintet. Carmen's drumming can also be heard on Pat Martino's latest CD entitled "Formidable" on the High Note label.

Carmen endorses Craviotto, DW, Sabian, ProMark, Evans and Lp products.

For more information please visit www.carmenintorrejr.com

Made in the USA
Columbia, SC
09 October 2024

43975223R00030